11-16-23

The Best in
Contemporary
Quilts

Coproduced by Lark Books
and The Dairy Barn Cultural
Arts Center

Lark Books
Asheville, North Carolina, USA

Quilt National Project Director: **Hilary Morrow Fletcher**
Editor: **Dawn Cusick**
Art Director: **Thom Gaines**
Photographer: **Brian Blauser**
Production Assistant: **Hannes Charen**

Additional photography provided by Image Inn (page 15), Anson Seale Photography (page 18), David Caras (page 24), David Beldo (page 32), Seth Tice-Lewis (pages 34 and 82), Mark Gulezian/Quicksilver (page 42), Bill Bachhuber (page 46), Pam Monfort (page 55 and 105), Roland Hueber (page 70), Peter Jenion (page 72), Zohar Zaled (page 79), Sharon Risedorph (page 84), Karen Bell (page 86), Ken Wagner (page 87), and Gerhard Heidersberger (page 98).

Library of Congress Cataloging-in-Publication Data
Quilt National (1999 : Athens, Ohio)
    The best in contemporary quilts: Quilt National, 1999, — 1st ed.
        p.   cm.
    "Coproduced by Lark Books and the Dairy Barn Cultural Arts Center."
    Includes index.
    ISBN 1-57990-110-7 (hard)
    1. Quilts—United States—History—20th century—Exhibitions.
    2. Quilts—History—20th century—Exhibitions.   I. Lark Books.
    II. Dairy Barn Southeastern Ohio Cultural Arts Center.   III. Title.
    NK9112.Q5   1999
    746.46'09'04907477197—dc21   99-13374
                                                           CIP

10 9 8 7 6 5 4 3 2 1

First Edition

Published by Lark Books
50 College St.
Asheville, NC 28801, US

©1999, Lark Books

Distributed by Random House,Inc.,in the United States, Canada, the United Kingdom, Europe, and Asia
Distributed in Australia by Capricorn Link (Australia) Pty Ltd., P.O. Box 6651, Baulkham Hills Business Centre,
    NSW 2153, Australia
Distributed in New Zealand by Tandem Press Ltd., 2 Rugby Rd., Birkenhead, Auckland, New Zealand

ISBN 1-57990-110-7

On the cover, a detail of *Collage II* by Sandra Altenberg.
On page 1, a detail of *In the Shallows* by Connie Scheele.
Opposite page from left to right, details of quilts by Ann Stamm Merrell, Dirkje vander Horst-Beetsma, Carol Taylor, and Linda Levin.

Contents

Miriam Nathan-Roberts

The Best in Contemporary Quilts

Foreword

As **Quilt National 1999** makes its debut, I find myself wondering what the Dairy Barn's Board of Trustees expected 20 years ago when the concept of an international competition and exhibition of innovative quilts was in its infancy. Did the founders of the newly established Dairy Barn Cultural Arts Center and of **Quilt National** think that the project would continue into the next millennium? Did they envision **Quilt National** as an event that would have world-wide impact? Did they realize that the day would come when there would be an automatic association between the words Dairy Barn Arts Center and **Quilt National**?

When one mentions the Statue of Liberty we know at once what it is and where it is. Likewise, the mention of **Quilt National** carries an immediate connection with The Dairy Barn Cultural Arts Center and Athens, Ohio. People who know what **Quilt National** is also know where it is, and this has become a source of pride for us.

We who are intimately involved with **Quilt National** have come to understand the importance of this biennial event. However, the statistics for this, the 11th **Quilt National**, tell an interesting story—one that could be appropriately entitled "More Than Ever Before...." The jurors for this **Quilt National** considered 1321 works from 637 artists. Nineteen percent of the entries came from 20 countries, including from Slovenia, Latvia, Russia, and South Korea for the first time. Forty-six percent of this year's entrants had not entered an earlier **Quilt National**. One-fourth of these, including some foreign artists, sent entry forms that had been downloaded from our site on the World Wide Web. The internet has obviously made the world a very small place.

This **Quilt National** collection is also among the largest with 86 works from artists from 27 states and 13 countries. Fifty-one percent of this year's artists are first-time exhibitors and more than one-fourth of the **QN '99** exhibitors are foreign. Jurors Nancy Crow, Caryl Bryer Fallet, and Bruce Pepich have shaped a diverse and exciting exhibit that bears witness to the strength of the creative energies of the world's artists. Although in some cases written and/or spoken communication requires the aid of a translator, it is quite clear that the languages of the medium and the art form are universal.

We look forward to welcoming the tens of thousands of visitors who will experience **Quilt National** here in Athens or at one of **QN's** many host venues. Fortunately, those who are unable to see **Quilt National** in person can gain an appreciation of the beauty, the diversity, and the technical expertise of the works through this book produced by the talented and wonderful people at Lark Books. We are most grateful to them for transforming the jurors' vision into a reality to be savored again and again by the readers.

I would also like to acknowledge the generosity and support of the many sponsors who have made ongoing and major commitments to **Quilt National**: the Fairfield Processing Corporation, maker of Poly-fil® brand fiber products;

Jane A. Sassaman

Quilts Japan magazine; VIP® Fabrics; Friends of Fiber Art International; Ardis and Bob James; Studio Art Quilt Associates; the Ohio Arts Council; the City of Athens; the Athens County Convention and Visitors Bureau; The Ohio University Inn; The Athens Messenger; Larry Conrath Realty; and several anonymous donors.

Jurors and sponsors, however, do not themselves make a show. The artists who so generously share their work with us are the final, and perhaps most critical, element. Viewing the entire body of entries for **Quilt National 1999** filled me with a sense of awe not only for the power of this medium, but also for the depth of talent that those works represented. It also provided me with a sense of comfort that a once-embryonic concept will surely continue to survive and mature for many years to come. We at the Dairy Barn Cultural Arts Center look forward to enabling that development and to sharing it with the rest of the world.

Susan Cole Urano
Executive Director
Dairy Barn Southeastern Ohio Cultural Arts Center

Introduction

When scientists study the evolution of a species, they often examine selected samples of a population and note the changes that occur over the passage of time. I believe that the size, diversity, and longevity of the **Quilt National** universe makes it a good population to study. By viewing the works in the 11 **Quilt Nationals**, we see the introduction and development of trends that not only characterize the art quilt of the '90s, but are likely harbingers of the art quilts we'll see in the next millennium.

Today's art quilt hasn't developed in a vacuum. Under the influences of history, technology, and the creative environment, art quilts have evolved to form a diverse body of work. These quilts represent the interaction of natural, social, and personal history with a multitude of materials and techniques and an endless depth of energy and imagination.

Before **Quilt National**, the word "quilt" nearly always referred to a particular kind of bed cover—a fabric sandwich. The layers were held together with thousands of tiny handmade stitches that complemented the design of the pieced or appliquéd top layer. When displayed on a bed, some of the quilt's surface was hidden, which meant that there was little point in creating a single, overall image. The quiltmaker's focus, therefore, tended to be on small-scale motifs that could be appreciated regardless of how much—or how little—the surface could be seen.

Then, in the 1970s, something happened that forever changed the nature of the quilt. Formally trained artists discovered an excitement in the exploration of repetitive patterns and in the technique of combining small bits of this and that. They took a new look at the humble quilted bed cover and began to view layered and stitched fabric as an attractive alternative to traditional art media. They saw endless possibilities in the colors and visual textures of cloth. They saw the stitched line as another source of design. And, perhaps most importantly, they escaped the tyranny of the quiltmaker's rules. They may not have known what a quilt should be, but they certainly knew what a quilt could be.

The result of this creative energy was a small body of work intended for walls rather than beds. It's not surprising that quilt show organizers and traditional quiltmakers felt threatened by these so-called artist-quiltmakers. Some of this work bore little apparent relationship to the warm, familiar creations people expected to see. "These objects aren't quilts!" the viewers announced. "They're art!"

At the same time, tools, and technologies were being developed that had the potential to create previously impossible effects. The new generation of sewing machines, color xerography, and readily available fabric paint and dyes presented challenges to which this new breed of quilt maker responded with gusto.

Yasuko Saito

Nancy Halpern once noted that she and "her kind" were considered mavericks in their quilt guilds. We are fortunate that the pioneers of the art quilt movement were not deterred by the disapproval of their early creations and that they courageously worked to produce quilts that differed from the familiar and accepted norms. They also encouraged others, by example, to begin creating highly personal and unique works.

Undoubtedly one of the most significant trends in the development of this art form is the use of surface design techniques—techniques that alter the color, pattern, and/or texture of the cloth. While generations of early quiltmakers selected fabrics on the basis of color or pattern, innovative quiltmakers were not content to limit themselves to the fabrics available in their local quilt shops. They wanted something other than a few solid colors and lots of calicoes, and they explored and employed a variety of techniques to create exactly what they needed.

By looking at works from all of the **Quilt National** exhibitions, we realize that today's quilts merge continuing traditions with new ones. Generations of quiltmakers, including contemporary artists, have taken advantage of differing visual textures of cloth. They have voiced concern

Heide Stoll-Weber

for social and personal issues. Added to these traditions are the relatively recent trends of using surface design techniques, of using materials and techniques that weren't available to earlier quilt-makers, of creating works for walls that may not be rectangular and may not even be solid, of manipulating the surface with something other than hand created stitches, and of producing images that may or may not be beautiful.

Fewer and fewer of today's innovative quilts are updated interpretations of classic quilt formats. The subject matter of the quilt, be it a personal memory or an artist's statement about a political or social issue, appears to be increasingly important. Today's artists view their quilts as a means of expressing their creative energies in ways that are

simply not possible with other materials. They are expanding and adding to the rich vocabulary of the heritage quiltmaker and they are transforming color and texture into dynamic patterns that provide new visual experiences.

There is no question that the art form has been enhanced by thousands of quiltmakers making personal journeys through explorations of color, shape, and line. I feel quite confident that through the continued creative efforts of the world's quiltmakers, the art quilt as we know it will continue to evolve and enrich the lives of an ever widening circle of appreciative viewers.

Hilary Morrow Fletcher
Quilt National Project Director

Jurors' Statements

Nancy Crow
Baltimore, Ohio

The phone call comes. The question is posed. The answer? "Yes, I would love to be a juror for **Quilt National '99**." It is so easy to say yes. But, in truth, accepting such an offer remains only an abstract idea that won't awaken until some future date. And since that date is so far off, anxiety does not erupt in uncomfortable vibrations until the date arrives.

On Friday afternoon, October 2, as I drove my van down through the Southeastern Ohio hills to Athens, I kept recycling...anxiously...the same thoughts ...1321 entries! So many entries! How can we possibly look at so many slides so rapidly in such a short amount of time? I tried to keep the thoughts of dozens of slide carrousels out of my mind and deliberately chose not to look at the stacks as I entered the jury room.

I wondered what those entries would look like 20 years after the first Quilt National '79. Every adjective came to mind as a possibility from fabulous, superb, and breath-taking to ridiculous, trite, and awful, then back to fresh, gutsy, and new. I hoped the entries would reflect the best of what is happening now, nearly 30 years since the contemporary movement surged forth and spread worldwide.

By 9:00 that evening, we three jurors were seated, ready for the initial overview. Carousel after carousel after carousel. No talking. What astounded me, considering how widely I travel when teaching, was how little of the work I recognized, including new work by known quiltmakers. I had worried that I would see far too many "workshop quilts" reflecting the teaching that Caryl and I do, but those percentages were not high.

What totally shocked me at this first viewing was the enormous amount of just bad photography. So many unprofessional slides. Too dark. Too light. Out of focus. Hey people, listen up: one does not photograph work draped over tables, sofas, railings, or clotheslines, or lying on rugs, grass, blacktops, gravel, or sidewalks, or up against dark paneling or busy wallpaper—and, most certainly, not with show ribbons attached! Has anyone heard of taping off slides? Or, better still, hiring a professional to do the job?

Hilary Fletcher, the long-time director of **Quilt National**, is a highly organized saint! She and her hard-working group of volunteers, including husband Marv, were always efficient, punctual, and ready to go, keeping a tight pace that allowed us to finish by the Sunday deadline. Marv Fletcher has devised a jurying process using computer technology that has made the Quilt

National system one of the fairest I have ever used. After being given instructions, we began. We sat apart, each with our own set of sheets. Hilary was immovable about not revealing any artist's name. We asked anyway, but got no answers. Silently we assigned each entry a number of 1 or 2 or 3, with 3 being high. The voting was kept totally secret. I never saw Caryl's or Bruce's sheets and never knew how they voted. The sheets were tallied after each round by a computer in another room. Because there was so much work to be seen, we had to keep pushing forward and stay focused.

I went to Athens fully expecting to see lots of new work testing boundaries out of outrageousness . . . parallel to what has been happening in other media. But in actuality, most entries stayed within the definition stated in the entry form. In 1979 and 1981, far more traditional quilts were entered than contemporary ones. This time, very few traditional quilts were entered.

What I did and have noticed is that quilts today have grown smaller in size. The first three Quilt Nationals were filled with works 7' x 7' or larger. Those quilts were conspicuous in their bold visual impact. They were meant to be seen from a long distance. And maybe they were large because they were still tethered to the idea of being bed quilts. Today, quilts are often more intimate in size and more complex in nature with abundant surface patterning. Technique often seems to be the only important aspect. But for many of us who have called this our medium for more than 20 years, I suspect the "visual wallop" was what attracted us to quiltmaking in the first place.

Hilary Fletcher, I congratulate you for your energy and focus in shaping and honing **Quilt National** into an impressive, world-recognized event. May **Quilt National '99** celebrate your nearly 20 years of love and dedication. Well done!

During the past 20 years, Nancy Crow's immeasurable talents have unequivocally established her as a giant in the contemporary art world. She wears many hats as trend-setter, master, and mentor. In addition to being the author of four books, Ms. Crow is the originator of Quilt National, the Quilt/Surface Design Symposium, and the Art Quilt Network. Her work is included in the permanent collections of many major museums, including the American Craft Museum and the Museum of American Folk Art. Among her many solo exhibitions is the recent exhibition at the Smithsonian Institution's Renwick Gallery in Washington, D.C. She has also designed many fabric collections that are marketed in retail outlets throughout the world.

Constructions #17 Cotton fabrics
hand dyed by artist; machine pieced (by artist), hand quilted (Marla Hattabaugh); 41 by 82 inches.

I began working on the *Constructions* series in earnest in late 1996 and plan to keep working on this series through 1999 and perhaps longer. I am highly influenced by architecture and in particular tall, vertical lines such as the tall, vertical beams in the timber-frame barns we have been renovating. The *Constructions* series is also about how to make parts that fit together into something whole.

Nancy Crow

Caryl Bryer Fallert

Oswego, Illinois

Several years ago I heard a famous dancer state that "One of the purposes of art is to move you, from where you are to someplace else." In 1983, when I was just beginning to make quilts myself, I saw a **Quilt National** exhibition for the first time, and it definitely moved me to someplace else. That show was full of quilts that expanded my idea of what a quilt could be in terms of materials, techniques, subject matter, shape, and presentation. Subsequent Quilt Nationals have continued to extend the boundaries of the medium.

I am continually amazed by the creativity of my fellow quilt makers. Just when you think you have seen and thought of everything that could possibly be done with "multiple layers of fabric, stitched through," along comes someone new who has looked at the quilt from a different point of view and added another dimension to our medium. In each **Quilt National**, I have also been personally inspired by the mature work of some of the master quilt artists among us, work that has grown beyond "let's try something different" to well thought out artwork that has a sophisticated blend of content, composition, and craftsmanship.

As a juror for this show, some of the questions I asked myself were: What kind of show is **Quilt National**? Is it a show about the outer fringes of the medium? Are we looking for shock value? Are we looking for a political or social point of view? Is it simply the best of the best of the work that is being done in the medium today? Is it a survey of as many of the different styles and concepts as possible? Ideally we would like it to be all of these things. The painful reality, however, was that we needed to choose just 84 quilts from 1321. Each of the quilts we chose has some, or all of the above qualities, as did a large percentage of the quilts that were not chosen.

As jurors, each of us naturally approached our decisions with a different set of personal aesthetic preferences. This, no doubt, is evident in our final choices. What we found we had in common was a belief in the importance of some universal artistic qualities in the work. Regardless of the timeliness of the subject matter or novelty of the artist's vision, we attempted to select quilts that embodied good design, composition, color choices, and craftsmanship.

In the course of the first two days of jurying, we viewed each of the 1321 quilts at least twice. One of the trends we noticed in the submitted slides was the very large number of randomly pieced, abstract compositions. After looking at literally hundreds of quilts in this style, the ones that had some kind of focus or overall compositional plan quickly distinguished themselves from the rest.

Naturally, quilts that were different in some way from all the others tended, at least initially, to capture our attention.

By late afternoon of the second day, we had selected the quilts we found the most compelling, that had some kind of overall visual or emotional impact. We had also relinquished many of the quilts we loved, from among groups of similar quilts, all of which had merit. By early evening, when we had hoped to have less than 125 quilts remaining, we still had 285 quilts, each of which we felt needed to be in the show. At this point, we voted one more time, indicating individually quilts we absolutely wanted in the show and quilts we felt we could sacrifice in order to reduce the number to a manageable size. When we saw the 125 quilts that remained, each of us found that some of our personal favorites were missing, and some we thought would be absent were still there. On the third day of jurying, we were able to discuss among ourselves the merits of individual quilts and come to a consensus. One of us, alone, could neither eliminate nor retain a quilt in the show. When the jurying process was over, we were surprised and delighted to discover that more than one-fourth of the final quilts were from outside the United States. I think the regional aesthetic qualities of these quilts enrich us all.

I am confident that the quilts we finally selected will provide viewers with a show to remember, full of joy and beauty, angst and uneasiness, laughter, wonder, awe, and lots of food for thought. My hope is that this show will move you, the viewer, to a new place, as past **Quilt Nationals** have done for me.

Caryl Bryer Fallert is internationally recognized for her award-winning art quilts. She is best known for her three-dimensional "high tech tucks" quilts and for her intricately pieced and densely quilted abstract and representational quilts. Her attention to detail has earned her a reputation for fine craftsmanship as well as stunning design. Ms. Fallert's works can be found in public, museum, corporate, and private collections in 22 states and six foreign countries. They have also appeared in hundreds of national and international publications and been displayed throughout North America, Europe, and Japan, as well as in Singapore, New Zealand, and Australia.

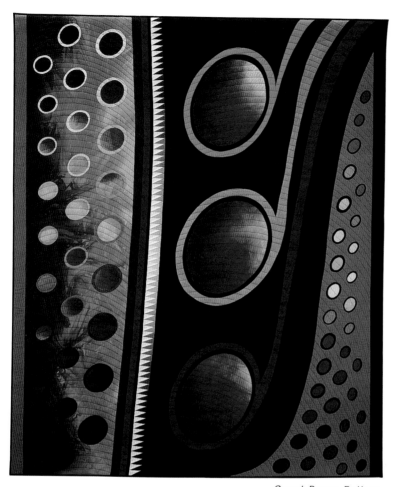

Caryl Bryer Fallert

Feather Study #1 Quilt top: 100% cotton fabric, fiber reactive dye, cotton and polyester thread, 100% wool batting, quilt back-commercial, whole cloth. Hand dyed, hand painted, machine pieced, machine appliquéd, and machine quilted; 78 by 65 inches.

When my husband and I moved to our Northern Illinois farm in 1978, we inherited a flock of guinea fowl. These comical birds gave us endless hours of entertainment. The feathers of the guinea fowl are highly patterned with black, white, and gray dots. The design for this quilt was inspired by a macro photograph of a single guinea feather. Of course, I took many artistic liberties with the colors of the feather, turning it into a graphic design that departs substantially from the original photographic inspiration.

Bruce Pepich
Racine, Wisconsin

Contemporary quiltmakers employ the fiber medium to form a synthesis between the compositional elements of painting and the technical perfection found in their craft. Today, when artists are trying to reach the widest possible audience with their work, quilts provide an effective bridge between formal, artistic concerns and the historic connotations of the medium. Quilts have a rich tradition of associations, including handwork, social activity, and the emotional and physical comfort coverlets have offered. These associations provide this contemporary art form with its attraction to creators and viewers alike.

As jurors, our daunting task was to select a group of just over 80 examples from a pool of hundreds of high-quality works. Slides are the only format possible for viewing and evaluating so large a number of large-scale artworks. And while the addition of detail images assists the juror in understanding the finer points of the way the artist has handled his/her materials, one does miss the tactile experience of handling each object. The best way I found to evaluate the entrants was a careful screening of the work's overall composition. As a two-dimensional work, I believe a quilt must have an effective composition and be well designed. It must clearly communicate the message for, as with any other work, content and message are extremely important. I sought works demonstrating a mastery of materials and techniques used to express an idea. No matter how interesting a work may be, if it is poorly fashioned or assembled, it misses its mark.

The next step was to interpret the idea that a work attempts to convey, whether it appears valid and how effectively it is communicated. The statement in a work may be simple, analogous to a short story, or complex, akin to a large novel or epic motion picture. A range of these messages brought together in the same group exhibition presents many different voices and a stimulating experience for the viewer.

The last—and most difficult—step in this process was the final round in which one must trim admired works from the entries to make the exhibition fit the space. By this time the show has been winnowed down to finalists, and the jurors must begin to eliminate pieces they personally prefer. This stage of the jurying involves intense comparison and evaluation. While it is frustrating to eliminate works one has come to admire, it is also an opportunity to refine the selections. This is the time when a competition is physically sculpted into the final exhibition.

Abstraction has been an important aspect of this medium. Historic crazy quilts, for example, predate most of the nonobjective painting of this century. The elaborate stitches in these works connect disparate pieces of fabric similar to the ways that line and color can be used to attach one collaged piece of paper to another. In these works, fabrics can be pieced to create illusions of natural space, while dyed and printed textiles are reminiscent of painted and washed passages of color. If stitches can be equated to the drawn line, the face of these textiles and their pieced application suggests the surface and texture of a painting.

As with many contemporary painting exhibitions, the greatest number of works in this show are abstract compositions. Many of these are based upon recognizable subject matter such as the figure, landscape, and still life from which the artist departs visually. These works become a forum in which depictions of the landscape deal with environmental issues, where the human figure leads to examinations of gender issues, and where still life serves as a comment on popular culture. However, the largest number of works in **Quilt National '99** are non-objective compositions drawing from the abstractions found in historic quilts. Some are organic, while others are geometric. Some works are subtly arranged, while many are brashly exuberant in their color and design. All delight in the use of fabric and stitching as a means of communication in much the same way as we see painters creating works that are about the act of pure painting and the making of marks.

Quilt National '99 also includes works that explore fiber technique and conventions. There are pieces whose construction materials and methods question how far a quilt can be altered before it no longer fits the definition of a quilt. The exhibition includes examples that examine the function of the supporting structure and the role it can have as a design element. The historic narrative role of quilts in an electronic and computerized culture is further explored by other exhibitors. The idea brought forth by these artists should serve as a discourse between the artists and viewers, which will continue to advance the field.

There was a high level of excellence seen in the entries in this year's competition. The technical ability, vision, and viewpoints presented by the exhibiting artists allowed the jurors to separate works that are unique and interesting during the jurying process. The attraction for me of working on juried competitions is the opportunity to discover new works, artists, and ideas on a firsthand basis. I thank all the artists who have entered **Quilt National '99** for this great opportunity.

Since 1981, Bruce W. Pepich has served as the director of the Charles A. Wustum Museum of Fine Arts in the tri-county area of Racine, Kenosha, and Lake Geneva, Wisconsin. Under his aegis, the museum has achieved a reputation for excellence through an active schedule of exhibitions that includes solo shows of emerging artists and mid-career surveys of important midwestern artists. Mr. Pepich is listed in the 18th edition of Who's Who in American Art. *In addition to being a frequent author, lecturer, and panel moderator, he has participated in over 40 jury panels for regional and national competitive art exhibitions and fine art fairs, including the prestigious Smithsonian Craft Show in Washington, D.C.*

From left to right, *details of quilts by Heide Stoll-Weber, Jane Burch Cochran, Ann Stamm Merrell, Maya Schönenberger, Judith Perry, Judy Hooworth, and Judy McDermott.*

The Quilts

Award of Excellence

Overlay 4 Hand-dyed and commercial cottons; screen printing, machine piecing, machine quilting; 54 by 54 inches.

Overlay 4 contrasts the rigidity of the grid and the controlled value gradation of the background with the playful unpredictability of irregular strip piecing.

Ruth Garrison
Tempe, Arizona

Maine/Frenchman's Bay II Synthetic fabrics treated with transfer dyeing, fabric overlays, and machine stitching; machine pieced, appliquéd, and quilted; 56 by 44 inches.

Maine/Frenchman's Bay II is part of a series inspired by a special place in northern Maine. I'm interested in the changeable quality of light and its effect on water, land, and sky.

Linda Levin
Wayland, Massachusetts

49 Vignettes on Turning 50 Dyed and pieced industrial wool felt; handstitched; 67 by 68 inches.

Memories of travel, encounters, and visions, including fragments
of baskets, woven cloth, quilts, landscapes, seasons, and textures
as I approach age 50.

Barbara Schulman
Kutztown, Pennsylvania

雅 Miyabi Japanese kimono silk; embroidered, hand and machine pieced, hand and machine quilted; 76 by 76 inches.

This is the reproduction of my parents' kimonos from about 70 years ago, which could have otherwise been thrown away. This work allowed my thoughts to fly back to the times when artisans carefully created those kimonos, thus reminding me of a sense of duty to pass a piece of history on to the next generation. In today's high-paced world dominated by technology, it is nice to know that at least something never changes.

Harue Konishi
Tokyo, Japan

Chroma Zones V Silk noil, fiber reactive dye, and potato dextrin resist (front) and hand-printed wax resist (back); appliqué and reverse appliqué by machine and machine quilted; 33 by 71 inches.

This quilt is one from a group I have made using a childhood puzzle as a design format for quilt blocks. The puzzle has ten pieces that can be arranged to create a square from a seemingly infinite number of solutions. In this composition the square of ten shapes has shifted into a flow where figure and ground mingle. I am investigating environmentally friendly dye resists. Vegetable resists, especially potato dextrin, wash out with water and make patterns unlike any other.

Ann M. Adams
San Antonio, Texas

18

Walmgate, November Hand-dyed, silk-screened, painted, and commercial cottons; fused (occasionally), machine pieced, and quilted; 51 by 64 inches.

Elizabeth Barton
Athens, Georgia

While walking through the old city (York, England) on a dreary November afternoon, I was struck by the warm yellow, amber, and pink glow of the windows. The contrast of the gold and gray, warmth and dank cold, and light and shadow reflected my own feelings of loss and sorrow, and — finally — peace.

Heartwood Commercial cottons and blends, hand-dyed and painted cottons, knitting material, rayon, silk, and cotton threads; machine pieced, appliquéd, and quilted; 60 by 37 inches.

Maya Schönenberger
Miami, Florida

Humans will always be part of nature. Similar to the growth of trees in the rain forest, where in regular cycles sapwood turns into heartwood and old, fallen trees turn into nurse trees, generation after generation of humans develop and change our world.

Back Yard: The Flats—Lowest Low Water Cotton fabric hand dyed by artist; hand pieced and hand quilted; 61 by 60 inches.

Pat Sims
Anchorage, Alaska

Living atop a 300-foot cliff overlooking Turnagain Arm of Cook Inlet, I am presented with views of arm's stunning seasons, tides, mountains, and skies. Part of an on-going series, *Back Yard: The Flats Lowest—Low Water* depicts a rare occurrence of the very lowest tide when tidal-pool depths expose primogenital sources.

Most Innovative Use of the Medium
sponsored by Friends of Fiber Art International

Cobblestones Commercial and hand-dyed cotton, silk, and polyester fabrics; freehand cutting, directly stitched on a foundation, and machine quilted; 52 by 61 inches.

Dirkje vander Horst-Beetsma
Tegelen, The Netherlands

My goal in playing around with fabric is to tell a story. This quilt is a walk in the garden on a sunny day. You see the colors of the flowers, shadows, trees, and the colors of the stones. The stones are old and can also tell us stories.

Requiem for an Ashtree Cottons (many Marimekko fabric scraps); machine pieced and machine quilted; 40 by 40 inches.

The battle of wills between the bold Marimekko fabrics from the 60s and my idea of a quilt was fought on my design wall while a beloved old ash tree was taken down after a slow death over a number of years.

Sylvia H. Einstein
Belmont, Massachusetts

Shattered Cotton fabrics dyed commercially and by the artist; machine pieced, quilted, and embroidered; 80 by 81 inches.

Nancy Crow's improvisational techniques have inspired my creativity and encouraged further experimentation with my own designs. A result of this experimentation is a quilt with a powerful electric center that emits charged black lines seeking to ignite combustible colors. Contact creates the illusion of a multicolored fabric explosion, as if tiny pieces of fabric are being ripped from the quilt, propelled toward the dark edges and blown onto the floor.

Carol Taylor
Pittsford, New York

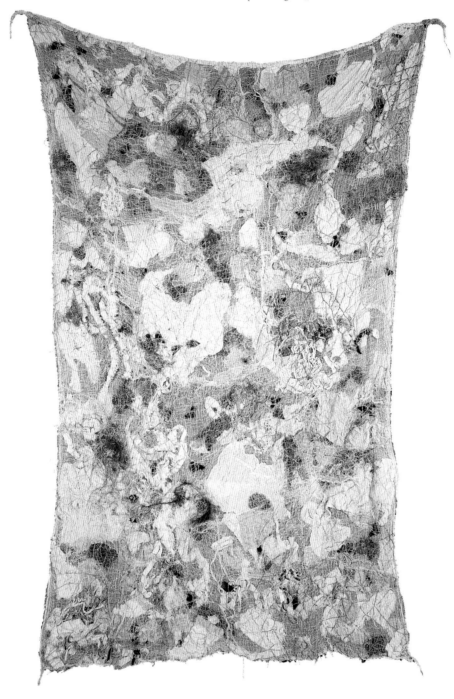

Lullaby II Found objects, discarded cloth, horsehair, and cheesecloth; hand embroidered and quilted;
50 by 78 inches.

Anna Torma
Hamilton, Ontario, Canada

I used all three essential layers of quiltmaking to build this piece. The batting is reused fabric and handwork between two layers of cheesecloth—loaded with textile making tradition. The handstitching is its skeleton, but also a visual part of the work. This is an unusual quilt, because normally invisible elements (batting and stitching) play a major role; in this quilt, though, the surface and backing are invisible. I did not use any expensive new material. This work is my visual/sensual statement about the beauty of waste.

Earth and Soul "To Go" Commercial cotton fabric, plastic, paper, and photographs shaped into plastic-stuffed biscuits, embellished with plastic covered pictures on earring wires; machine quilted; 42 by 56 inches.

Pat Owoc
St. Louis, Missouri

Plastic, it's everywhere! When we're done with it, we throw it away and it becomes permanent landfill. Plastic also denotes meaninglessness, stiff, false. How much of our world, both physical and spiritual, is plastic? Are we sealing off earth, humanity, and belief in plastic-covered "to go" bundles?

Sea Goddess Tapestry and drapery fabrics; fused, pieced, machine appliquéd, machine stitched; 43 by 27 inches.

Janis V. Jagodzinski
Baltimore, Maryland

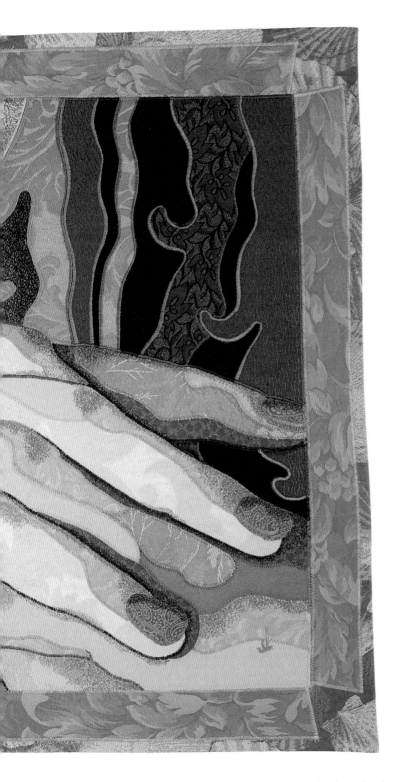

Sea Goddess is a mystical mermaid waiting near the shore, her body nestled between rocks and boulders as waves lick against jagged cliffs. Gazing out at the ocean, she anxiously awaits her lover's return from a distant voyage. Seaweed tangled in her hair, cool blue lips smiling in anticipation of his arrival. Chin propped on clasped hands, dreaming of the future they may someday share, and silently praying for his safe journey home.

Flow VI Cotton and silk organza fabrics painted with pigment; machine appliquéd, hand embroidered, hand and machine quilted; 39 by 46 inches.

This work developed out of a personal history of creating artwork that addresses structure, growth, and connections through surfaces composed of small, torn squares and rectangles. The emphasis in my current work is on the painted surface (versus directing the work through construction methods). I want to "see what's happening," rather than to direct "something to happen." Simple structure is balanced with painted and stitched surfaces, allowing the elements of simplicity and complexity to coexist. *Flow VI* continues my series referencing "being with the moment."

Erika Carter
Bellevue, Washington

African Violets 100% cotton and frayed chiffon fabrics, metallic thread; discharge dyed, painted, and machine quilted with free-motion style; 50 by 55 inches.

Rosanna Lynne Welter
Salt Lake City, Utah

I am currently consumed with contrast and texture. Discharge dyeing, which I use extensively, is perfectly suited to create high-contrast fabrics. I added further contrast to *African Violets* by simply positioning lines against curves. The quilting of primitive/geometric images over the entire surface, along with raw edges and hanging threads, created extensive texture and ultimately defined this piece. My goal was to create dimension and movement away from a flat wall.

Best of Show

Spin Cycle Commercial and hand-dyed, hand-painted, and airbrushed fabrics; machine appliquéd and machine quilted; 66 by 71 inches.

Miriam Nathan-Roberts
Berkeley, California

This quilt is the latest in the *Interweave Series* started in January 1983. Every time I finish one I think it is the last of that series, but then yet another beckons me. I have been interested in structure and illusions of depth all my life. My father was interested in bridges, and Pittsburgh (where I grew up) is a city of bridges. He often pointed out the differences in their structures to me. I have no real depth perception because my eyes don't achieve fusion (one is near-sighted and the other is far-sighted.) Most of the fabrics were hand dyed by me. All of the pieces were individually airbrushed by me. The quilt was named by my friend Nancy Halpern.

The Chevy: '57 Bel Air Coupe Commercial and hand-dyed cotton fabrics; machine-stitched raw-edge appliqué with machine quilting; 76 by 90 inches.

Alice Norman
Boise, Idaho

Intrigued by the design possibilities of the raw-edge appliqué technique, I chose a subject with complex planes, transparent elements, and highly reflective surfaces. For the first glance, I wanted the image to convey the spirit and romance of this popular model, compelling viewers to step closer to examine details. In 1950's America, this car epitomized the "baseball, apple pie, and Chevrolet" slogan for social optimism.

Rolling Toys Whole cloth quilt, hand dye-painted with Procion dyes and acrylic paints; machine quilted; 54 by 48 inches.

Happy, playful images come into my mind when I think of the children in West Africa. Tires provide hours of endless pleasure and are perhaps the most common toy.

Hollis Chatelain
Hillsborough, North Carolina

Yon and Beyond Hand-dyed and commercial fabrics; machine pieced and hand quilted; 51 by 48 inches.

On a spring 1998 trip to South Africa I traveled about 4,000 miles by car, and the beautiful directional arrows on the pavement were the inspiration for this motif. The colors of Northern Arizona inspired the colors.

Marla Hattabaugh
Scottsdale, Arizona

35

Discourse Hand-dyed Pima cotton, muslin, and cotton sateen fabrics; machine pieced, appliquéd, and quilted; 63 by 25 inches.

Judith Anton
Wardsboro, Vermont

This work begins and ends with the fabric. My technique is called "sliding." I place fabrics over and under each other and slide them until I begin to feel the direction to take. No sketch was used in forming the basic concept. This way of working gives me complete freedom in creating the piece. It gives the fabric placement "maximum flow," by allowing the colors, textures, and shapes to bounce off each other, thereby creating the piece's own energy.

Night Fliers A wide variety of new and recycled fabric, ribbon, and found materials that were machine collaged and embellished with paint; machine pieced, appliquéd, and quilted; 72 by 57 inches.

Nancy Gipple
Afton, Minnesota

Night Fliers is one of a series of pieces inspired by watching my young niece and nephew draw. I was so impressed with the open and spontaneous nature of their approach. The preciousness was in the freedom of an open and spontaneous mind-set, not in the preciousness of the material goods or in a rigid perfection of technique. To me, the most meaningful work is when I find this same attitude in the quilt tradition. Watching them freed me, if just for a moment.

Collage II Silk tissue and fabric that was hand dyed, painted, glued, and stitched; hand and machine pieced and stitched; 15 by 18 inches.

Sandra Altenberg
Seattle, Washington

I was challenged creatively by working within the two-layer requirement for this show. I developed a way of bringing together this tissue, fabric, and stitching as one texture and surface. This was accomplished through a process of dyeing, painting, and layering the materials. I then utilized piecing techniques in reconstructing the materials into this unique composition.

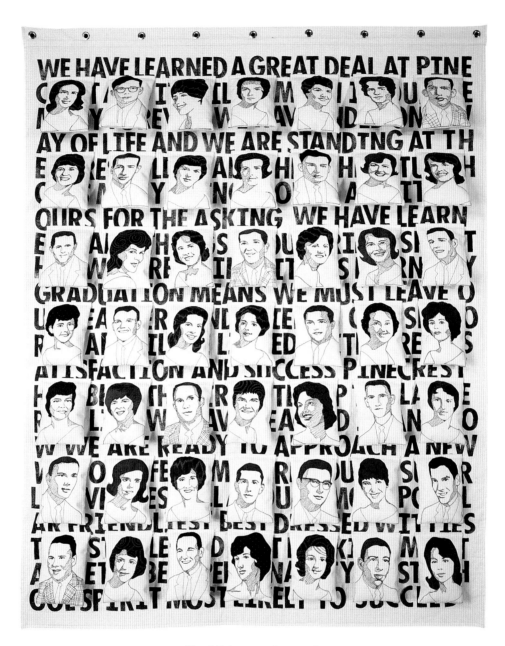

Dreams Artist canvas, fused cotton fabric, and candlewick thread; free-motion machine stitchery, hand and machine quilting; 48 by 60 inches.

Faye Anderson
Boulder, Colorado

It is not that encouraging to be voted Most Talented in a high school that didn't offer a single art class, but at age 17 the gap between fantasy and reality doesn't seem that wide. There's a lot of room to dream, and sometimes the dreams do come true. This quilt was created in a reflective mood. I haven't been in touch with anyone from the PineCrest class of '63 for many years, but I enjoyed rereading their yearbook quips and notes while stitching the portraits, and hope that they have shared my good fortune. *P.S. Those who wrote that they didn't think that I was all that talented somehow vanished between the worktable and the sewing machine.*

Chaim's Tree Hand-dyed and discharged cottons; machine pieced and machine quilted; 26 by 34 inches.

Chaim's Tree grew out of a love for nature. The circular forms that are the "trunk" of my tree honor nature lessons learned from watching my garden grow, bloom, freeze, and reemerge to bloom anew. The title, however, blossomed only after the piece was quilted. The Hebrew word for life is *chaim* and it was also my grandfather's name. This tree of life is dedicated to him.

Malka Dubrawsky
Austin, Texas

41

Red Landscape 2 Cotton and silk fabric treated with textile paint, fiber reactive dye, and Theox (discharge) paste; monoprinted, screenprinted, machine appliquéd, and machine quilted; 61 by 40 inches.

Dominie Nash
Bethesda, Maryland

Color and texture are the dominant elements in my work. This piece is an exploration of the interaction of large areas of subtly textured saturated color with graphically patterned black and white sections. The color becomes more emphatic by contrast, while the black-and-white patterning compensates for the absence of color.

Tumbling Reds 100% cotton hand dyed by Heidi Stoll-Weber; machine strip pieced, machine strip quilted in quilt-as-you-go technique; 60 by 60 inches.

Judith Larzelere
Belmont, Massachusetts

I see myself as one of many artists working in a medium that was once considered only a craft, and a woman's craft at that. I struggle to use all the basic tools of art and design theory, but I express myself with fabric rather than pigment on canvas. I make images that would be next to impossible to create with paint, but can quite easily be accomplished using the techniques natural to cloth, such as cutting apart and reconnecting with thread.

43

Passing Harbin's Cotton blends and recycled fabrics; machine pieced, painted, appliquéd, embroidered, and hand quilted; 60 by 37 inches.

Anne Smith
Warrington, Cheshire, England

Harbin's was an old textile mill in my home town. I used to pass it every Sunday and peep through a gap in the big wooden door to see and smell the machinery. As I grew up, the old door decayed and then disappeared, along with the mill.

Irregular Thought Patterns Hand-dyed and commercial cottons and silks; machine appliquéd onto canvas and machine quilted; 39 by 39 inches.

I do not like lines that are exactly parallel. I do not understand junctions that are entirely smooth. I have not experienced many journeys of note in which it was revealed early on what the final destination would be.

Sally A. Sellers
Vancouver, Washington

Aquifer Cotton fabrics that have been hand dyed and painted by the artist; fused and machine quilted; 25 by 27 inches.

Aquifer is part of a series based on cracked pavement, which became pathways and rock walls. The fabric I dye sometimes develops air bubbles which can look three dimensional when cut away from the whole. These "rocks" were piled into pastel geological formations and layered between sunrise skies.

Melody Johnson
Cary, Illinois

The Best in Contemporary Quilts

Juror's Award of Merit

Agape Cotton fabric shibori dyed with Procion dyes, some discharged; machine pieced and machine quilted; 60 by 52 inches. On loan from a private collection.

Jan Myers–Newbury
Pittsburgh, Pennsylvania

My dyeing techniques continue to be relatively primitive with gradual changes and an occasional lurch forward, always in the context of what I have done before. Discoveries made while creating one piece generate a starting point for the next. The depth and beauty of the fabrics excite and inspire the design. Agape is a Greek word for love, referring to the love that extends outward and is freely given, the grace of God.

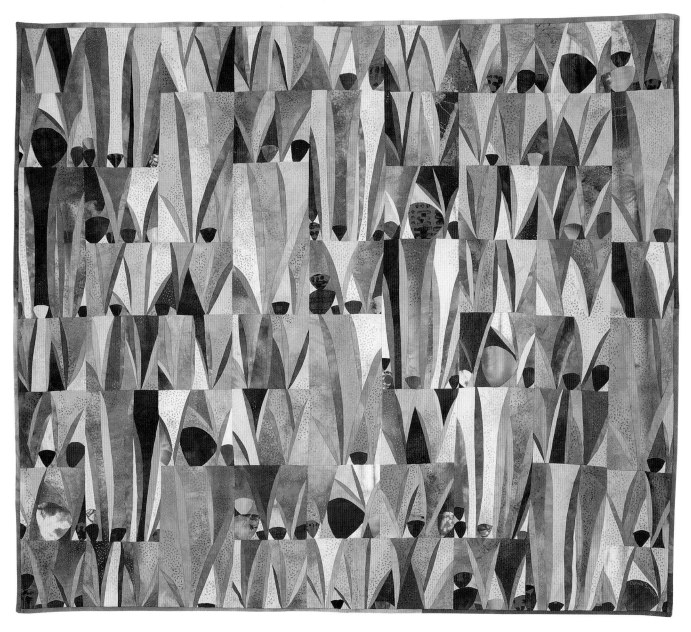

Domini McCarthy Award

In the Shallows Hand-dyed cottons; machine pieced and hand quilted; 53 by 46 inches.

After doing a number of *River Rocks* quilts, I did a few quilts of foliage and grasses. This quilt is an integration of the two, and is reminiscent of the northern Wisconsin lake country that is very important to me.

Connie Scheele
Houston, Texas

Breaking Ground Hand-dyed cottons and commercial fabrics; machine pieced and machine quilted; 56 by 56 inches.

After a devastating fire destroyed my next-door neighbors' house, I looked out of my studio window at an ash-covered lot for 18 months. Finally, work began to rebuild the house. I started the quilt *Breaking Ground* the day the construction equipment moved onto the lot and started moving ground for the house foundation.

Janet Steadman
Clinton, Washington

Primitive Door Series – VIII Keep Out Canvas, cotton, acrylic paint, various threads; machine thread painted and machine quilted; 27 by 29 inches.

Vita Marie Lovett
Marietta, Georgia

In the foothills of the Tennessee Smoky Mountains, in an area known as Piney Branch, I came upon a weathered barn with a "Keep Out" warning. Barns are a landmark of rural America that are fast on their way to disappearing. These old structures have inspired me to create vignettes of the past through fabric and thread.

Celtic Crosses 3.1, 3.2, 3.3 Cotton, silk, linen, and blend fabrics, screen door netting, old embroidered tablecloth, patchwork from my Great Aunt Lena Tomlinson; fused and machine stitched; 22 by 21 inches, 21 by 23 inches, 24 by 22 inches.

Ann Stamm Merrell
Cupertino, California

The construction method for these abstract Celtic crosses involves starting with squares of fabric and going through several iterations of cutting, swapping, and sewing, without any predetermined outcome. In this case I started out with 24 pieces of fabric, each associated in some way with the Trinity: the color red for Sustainer/Holy Spirit, schools of fish for Creator/God, a cross for Redeemer/Jesus, or by some unarticulated feeling of mine.

The Teapot/High Priestess (Card #2 of The Kitchen Tarot) Fabric, beads, gemstones, Mardi Gras beads, shells, buttons, antique jewelry, and assorted collectibles and found objects; painted, airbrushed, embroidered, appliquéd, quilted, and embellished by hand; 87 by 55 inches.

This piece is the third quilt of *The Kitchen Tarot*. In this quilt, Susan's invented saint, St. Quilta the Comforter, makes her first appearance in the deck. She wears an entire teapot (instead of her usual tiara of a Fiestaware teacup), which is in the top of the quilt now. She has her ever-present Lucky Tomato Pincushion. (Whenever one is around a room, St. Q can spontaneously manifest!)

Susan Shie
and James Acord
Wooster, Ohio

Je t'aime Fabric, beads, buttons, paint, clothing, gloves, gold leaf, color pencil, china markers, pastels, playing cards; machine pieced, hand appliquéd with beads, embellished, and monoprinted; 63 by 60 inches.

The working title for this quilt was *Nearly New*, a term referring to used clothing in good condition. I started intuitively putting images together from materials I had collected and received as gifts (in this quilt special thanks to Betsy Cannon, Anita Corum, and Beth Kennedy). I made a monoprint from the blouse and rickrack glove, using the originals as plates and acrylic paint to print. Suddenly I realized the quilt was just a big old nine patch about romantic love. I had found a handkerchief that said both *I love you* and the beautiful French companion *Je t'aime*. It is in the painted denim pocket in the upper right corner.

Jane Burch Cochran
Rabbit Hash, Kentucky

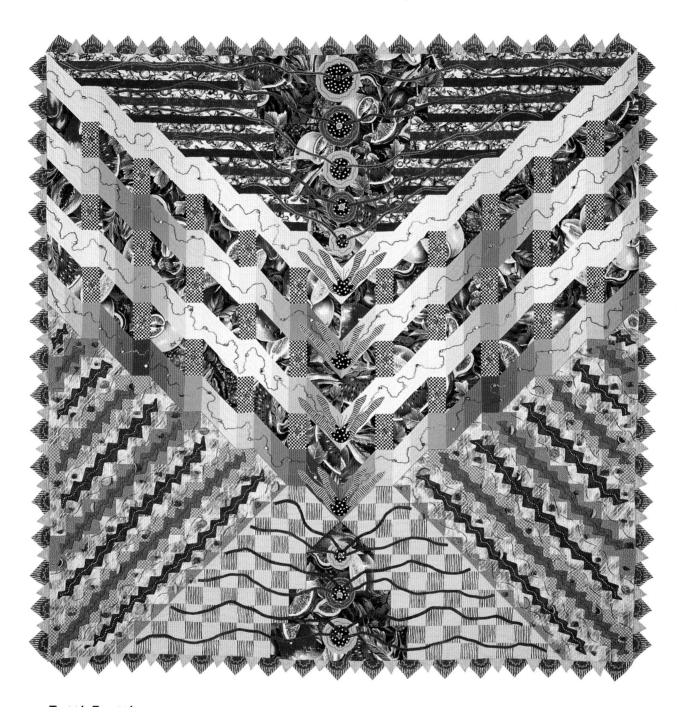

Tutti Frutti Various materials including cotton fabric, embroidery floss, buttons, beads, chenille fiber, and perle cotton; machine pieced, hand quilted, hand appliquéd, hand embroidered; 72 by 72 inches.

This piece represents the rich cornucopia of life choices the world offers us. Though there may be many twists and turns in this "mixed salad," if you really want to, you can find a way to accomplish anything. All your opportunities are there in front of you for the tasting. Open your eyes, reach out, pick one, take a bite, sieze the day!

Jill Pace
Glendale, Arizona

Floral Symphony #2: Foxgloves Hand-dyed cottons and discharge-dyed polyester computer transfers; machine pieced, appliquéd, and quilted; 24 by 29 inches.

Barbara Barrick McKie
Lyme, Connecticut

As a photographer and former computer consultant, I have been experimenting with computer fabrics since 1994. Realistic images from my photographs become computer-disperse dye transfers. Abstract backgrounds and semirealistic parts of the design are my hand-dyed fabrics. Themes involving nature and still lives are my usual, though not exclusive, subject matter. Foxgloves in my cousin's garden inspired *Floral Symphony #2: Foxgloves*, the second in a series of floral studies.

Wisteria Cottons and blends; machine pieced, hand appliquéd, and hand quilted; 88 by 88 inches.

In Japan, the wisteria are now in full bloom every spring. The purple flowers and fresh, verdurous leaves are beautiful swaying in the wind. This quilt is one picture of scenery in Japan.

Kuniko Saka
Tokyo, Japan

Hamsa Silks, velvets, embroideries, and embellishments; hand appliquéd, embroidered and quilted; 36 by 46 inches.

I trained as a painter and art teacher, arriving from abstract oil paintings to mixed media collage. When I felt the need to look back into my past, I realized that I could express my "Childhood Memories" of Iraq only in a textile medium. To me, composition takes the lead, while the colors and textures follow on.

Sara Nissim
Ramat-Gan, Israel

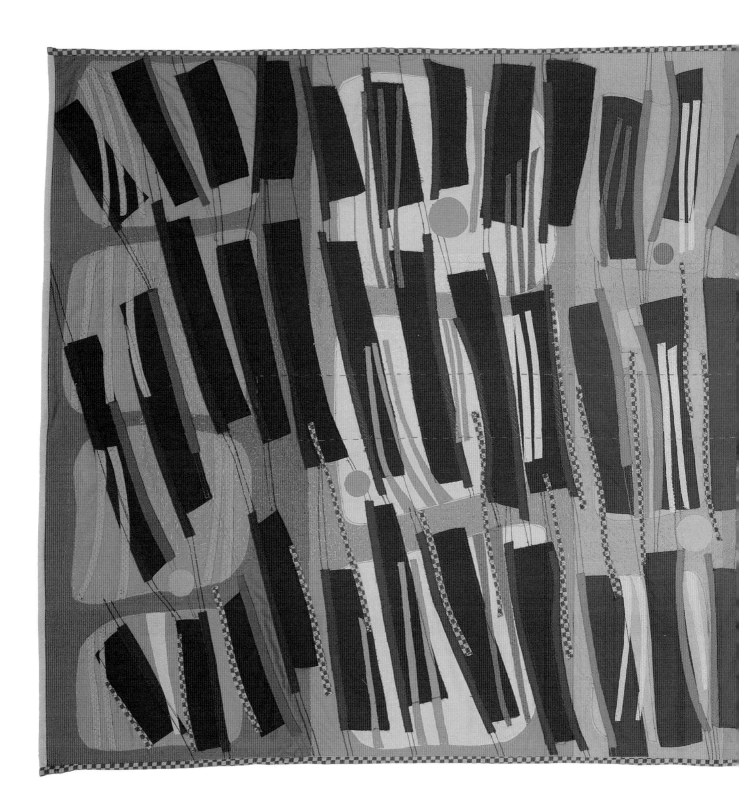

Trick Track Commercial hand-dyed cotton/poly fabrics; direct appliquéd, fused, embroidered, hand and machine stitched; 58 by 35 inches.

Jane Lloyd
Ballymena, County Antrim, Northern Ireland

60

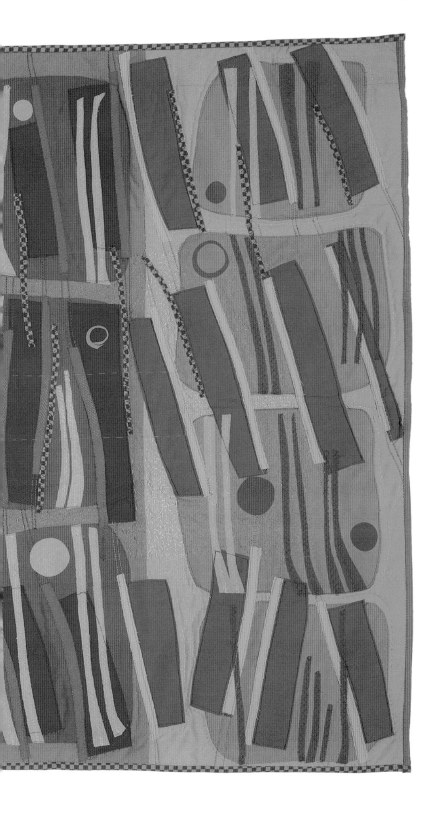

Treating the fabric like paper collage gave me great design freedom, thus
making it more exciting to create. I liked the idea of using large seeding
stitches to form a different texture and embroidery emphasizing some parts.

Garden Fantasy

Cotton fabrics hand dyed by
the artist and Kathy Sorenson
and/or painted by the artist
with metallic pens; machine
pieced and machine quilted;
54 by 56 inches.

Dirt doesn't hold my dreams –
Fabric does –
Flowers seen in splendor and brilliance –
Leaves and dragonflies –
Butterflies and birds –
Sunshine and moon glow –
All this and more –
My garden fantasy.

Judith H. Perry
Wilmette, Illinois

In Perspective Cotton fabrics; machine pieced, hand appliquéd, and hand quilted; 57 by 57 inches.

My inspiration for this particular piece was my favorite Johannes Vermeer painting, *A Lady at the Virginal with a Gentleman (The Museum Lesson)*. I tried to capture and use in my own way the palette of colors and the way the light streams in the open window, letting the golden light settle on the objects inside the room. And I thank Her Majesty, Queen Elizabeth II, for letting me see this painting at the National Gallery in Washington, D.C.

Anne McKenzie Nickolson
Indianapolis, Indiana

Quilts Japan Prize
sponsored by *Quilts Japan* magazine

Seeds and Blossoms Hand-printed fabric; machine appliquéd and machine quilted; 43 by 43 inches.

We have a dense garden in our small city yard. Every year we grow several varieties of angels' trumpets, also called jimsonweed or thorn apple. This plant is poisonous, yet incredibly dramatic. It has huge, white, sweet-smelling trumpet blossoms, dusty gray-green leaves, and wonderfully evil-looking prickly seed balls the size of Christmas ornaments. I absolutely love them so it was an obvious subject for a quilt.

Jane A. Sassaman
Chicago, Illinois

Print Series: "Her Very Own #5" 100% pima cotton fabric; direct appliqué machine stitched
to hold all layers together; 36 by 36 inches.

Barbara W. Watler
Hollywood, Florida

A decision to try a series of quilts using only black and white
focused my attention on fingerprints. Each fingerprint is a
unique and identifying design appealing to my need to never repeat a design. Examining my own prints proved
how quickly everyday tasks would subtly overlay the print design. Because I do hand stitching without a thimble,
several of my own prints have distorted, torn skin patterns, depending on which fingers print and which hand I
used for a particular quilt. When hung all together, this series of 20 machine-stitched quilts has an ebb and flow
of line and rhythm that reminds me of music.

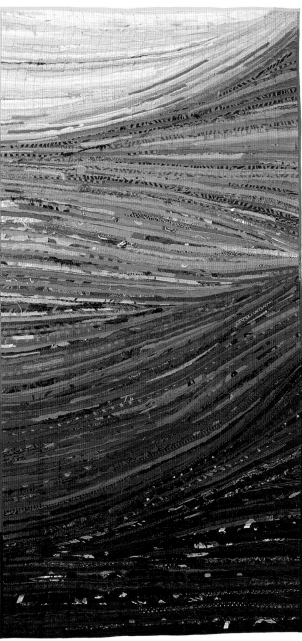

Mothers/Daughters #6 . . . Lines of Communication Cotton blends, torn fabrics;
layered and machine stitched to cotton batting, machine quilted; 78 by 78 inches.

Family relationships are fragile at times of stress and emotional upheaval. The bond between mother and daughter is
stretched to the fracture point. To help preserve a special and
loving relationship, the lines of communication, though tenuous, need to be kept open.

Judy Hooworth
Terrey Hills, New South Wales, Australia

Movement #4 Commercial and hand-dyed fabrics, some treated with paint; 81 by 74 inches.

The vision of the third millennium: In one moment all the stages of life are connected to 3,000 worlds. All existence in the universe is connected to and affected by each other fundamentally, deep down at the roots. And thus, an eternal harmony ultimately results from the cycle of life and death. White lines are the symbol of one such universe. I believe we could be the source of the harmony rather than chaos.

Yasuko Saito
Tokyo, Japan

Hand Tools Hand-dyed and commercial fabrics (cotton, silk, and wool), cotton, polyester, and metallic threads, acrylic paint; machine embroidery using a boil-away stabilizer, photo transfer, appliqué, and machine stitching; 75 by 46 inches.

B. J. Adams
Washington, D. C.

Machine embroidered hands are part of a theme in an ongoing series of my work. *Hand Tools* is an homage to creativity. The hands are created in a variety of colors and techniques to illustrate the varieties of people in our world. The tools are a small representation of the diversity of vocations and avocations available.

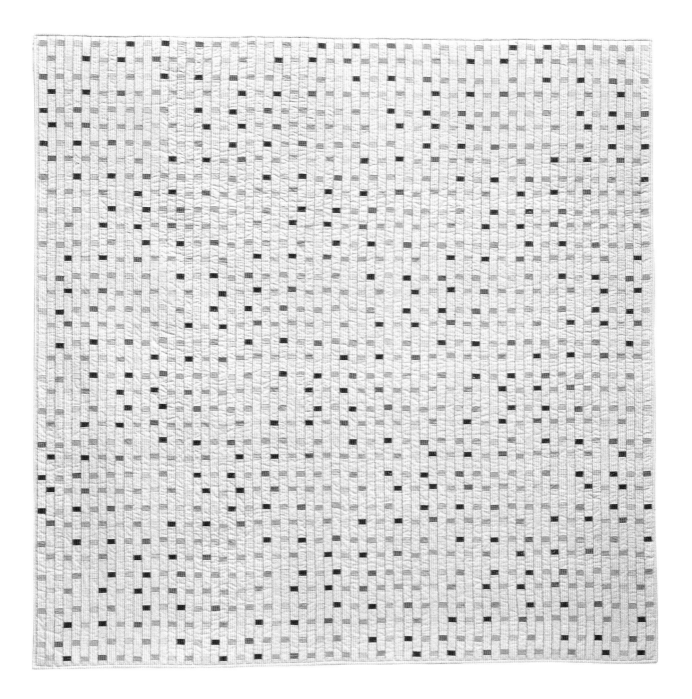

Ikat Quilt / Rhythm II Hand-dyed cotton; machine pieced and machine quilted; 79 by 78 inches.

This is an attempt to transform one old textile technique (ikat weaving) into another (piecing and quilting). I enjoy the contrast between a rigid concept and the floating pattern of the 11 rainbow colors.

Inge Hueber
Köln, Germany

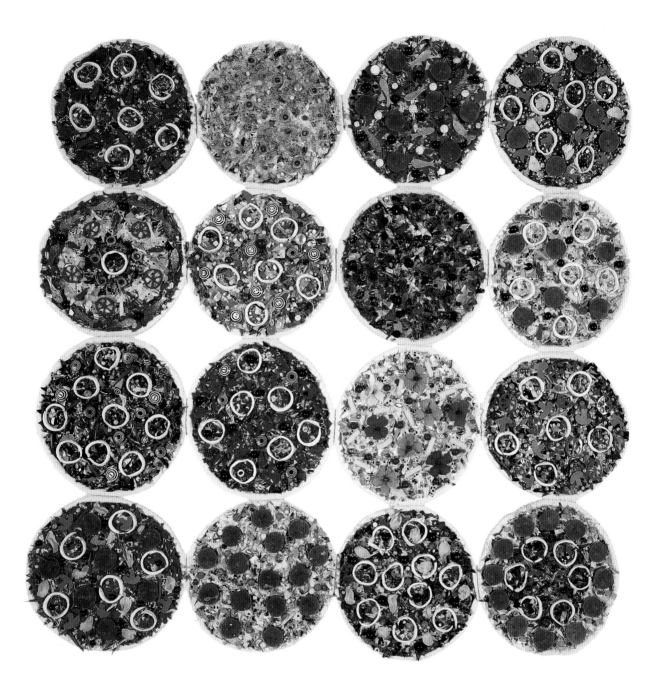

Laissez–les Manger du ~~Gâteau~~ Pizza Assorted materials including fabric, thread, buttons, rubber, wire mesh, leather, silk flowers, plaster, beads, and wood; machine stitched and hand quilted; 52 by 52 inches.

Donna Leigh Jackins
Birmingham, Alabama

Pizzas! They came to me in the middle of the night. Lately I've been traveling extensively with my husband, and the pizzas with ingredients are quite portable compared to the larger quilts I had been transporting. While sewing feta cheese in the Tokyo airport, I had a conversation with a Japanese quilter. She spoke no English. I spoke no Japanese. I've no idea what she said except for the word "pizza."

Appletreefield Silk and cotton fabrics, some hand dyed; direct and reverse appliqué, slashing, hand and machine stitching; 54 by 54 inches.

Elizabeth Brimelow
Macclesfield, Cheshire, England

Landscape is my inspiration. I study its history, archaeology, geology, and botany. I am interested in man's mark on it and the results of such interventions as mining, quarrying, building, ploughing, planting, and harvesting. Landscape is where I live, what I look at, what I draw, and what I stitch.

The Best in Contemporary Quilts

Reflections Hand-dyed polyester fabrics, silk-screening (pigments), bleach discharge with resists; machine stitched; 12 by 21 inches.

I am currently exploring silkscreen prints and various methods of discharging color. The initial surface choice affects these processes immensely. Here, the organic softness of the discharged cloth is the perfect complement to the hard-edge, printed image, although the very similar colors were arrived at by very different methods.

Barbara Bushey
Ann Arbor, Michigan

73

J. C. Raulston Arboretum Cotton fabric with each piece cut from individually designed plastic templates that are positioned as appropriate to the pattern in the cloth; machine pieced and hand quilted; 57 by 57 inches.

Ann Harwell
Wendell, North Carolina

A rainy June walk in the arboretum: down green-walled paths, over stepping stones to a water garden, hopping among the fish, frogs, and toads . . . past sculptures that evoke a sensual, spiritual freedom to a huge wicker dome entwined by red flowering vines and lorded over by raucous birds Under your feet is a tiled floor depicting trees with interlaced limbs.

Cacophony Silk necktie fabric; machine pieced and hand quilted; 55 by 55 inches.

On the wall of my studio there is pinned a quotation from Proust: "Be regular and orderly in your life, so that you may be violent and original in your work." I had been madly and obsessively slashing, stitching, and constructing this piece during a rather disruptive period when I realized that the grid and quilting of the Log Cabin block formation exemplifies that order and regularity. The rest . . . well, the rest speaks for itself.

Marjorie Hoeltzel
St. Louis, Missouri

Money for Nothing Sugar packets, nylon window screening, dental floss (mint flavored), green paper, and plastic flies; 73 by 33 inches.

John W. Lefelhocz
Athens, Ohio

Money is a strange force to be dealt with, and this force is in us rather than in the tactile paper and coins. Here's where I tell you what this piece is supposed to mean . . . Well, not really . . . I hope that you reach your own conclusions. I just make it, I don't define it. If I could define it, I wouldn't have to make it.

Le Labrynthe de Merlin Antique linen and hemp, hand spun and hand woven during the 19th-century in France and hand dyed by the artist; hand/machine pieced, appliquéd, and top stitched; 62 by 60 inches.

My first creative quilt in 1985 was a very tame, geometric labyrinth ... and my last quilt is still a labyrinth, but now it has reached a free dynamic and spontaneous folly. Why this fascination? Does the labyrinth represent a journey of initiation? A mysterious image slow to decipher? Or a magic positive-negative interplay? Another magic is added by my hand-dyed antique linen attesting to the touching work of our ancestors.

Anne Woringer
Paris, France

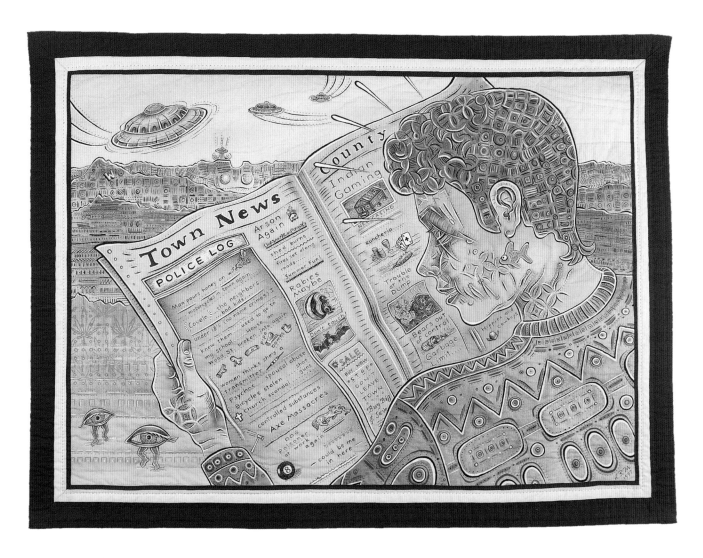

Town News Cotton fabric and batting; fabric is airbrushed, dyed, painted and hand quilted; 40 by 30 inches.

I live in a small town and every week the whole town reads the police log in the newspaper. It's a source of great entertainment. We read mainly about minor crimes, looking for people we know yet hoping we won't find our own or our family's names in there. While we are so myopic about the trivial pastimes of our fellow townees, I wonder if something truly amazing happened, such as spaceships landing on our mountain range, whether we would even notice. The items in the police log have happened in our town; we do have a hidden economy in the hills; and this is a self-portrait of me wearing my goldfish earrings and a surface designed t-shirt that has since worn out.

Linda MacDonald
Willits, California

Juror's Award of Merit

Relief Hand-dyed cotton from the artist's dye studio; machine pieced and machine quilted; 74 by 52 inches.

Like all my work, this quilt is a study in color and light. I start laying out most of my composition on a flannel-covered wall and keep adding details while I'm piecing. The whole process is very satisfying: it's like painting with hand-dyed fabrics.

Heide Stoll-Weber
Frankfurt, Germany

A Real Pretend Wagga For Paul Klee Wool/acrylic and wool fabrics; machine pieced and hand quilted with hand-dyed silk thread; 48 by 32 inches.

Judy McDermott
Thornleigh, Australia

This quilt is all about color. What to do with the ferocious orange from the op-shop? Add greens, as did Klee in his color studies. The yellow "makes the orange sing," says Johannes Itten, author of *The Art of Colour*. A wagga is a traditional Australian quilt or bush blanket made from wheat bags, old clothes, or found scrap materials. Many are roughly cobbled together, although my favorite is "sewn" with wire.

The Empty Tomb Various fabrics and found objects including velvet, polyesters, organza, glass beads, photo transfers and mirrors; hand and machine stitched and quilted; 96 by 90 inches. On loan from a private collection.

The void as the epicenter of God's creative activity . . . out of the tomb/womb comes transformation.

Sherri Wood
Carrboro, North Carolina

82

Obsessed Commercial fabrics; machine stitched; 47 by 61 inches.

Scraps on my table and my new sewing machine in the midst. Trying out my new toy, putting together the scraps around me without thinking about what I am doing, sewing for hours just for fun . . . what an adventure! When looking at the result of my obsession the next morning, I suddenly realized I had created something unique the night before — the birth of this work.

Ursula Baumung
Stutensee, Germany

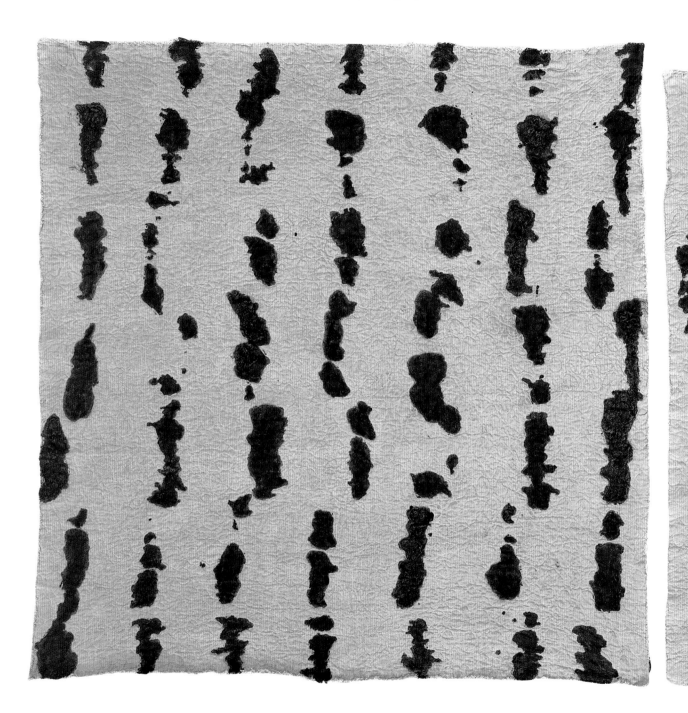

Binary Zen Hand-dyed linen, monoprinting; machine quilted; 108 by 56 inches.

This piece is from a series, *Skillful Means/Binary Zen*, that explores monoprinting on linen. I wanted to use a simple technique that would convey a meditative quality in the midst of turmoil. The 0s and 1s represent the complexities of life in the digital age. The term "skillful means" is often used by Buddhists to describe various methods of teaching; here it refers to the attempt to discover simplicity in seemingly complex patterns. This particular piece represents emptying, from a solid pattern of 1s to an all encompassing 0.

Suzan Friedland
San Francisco, California

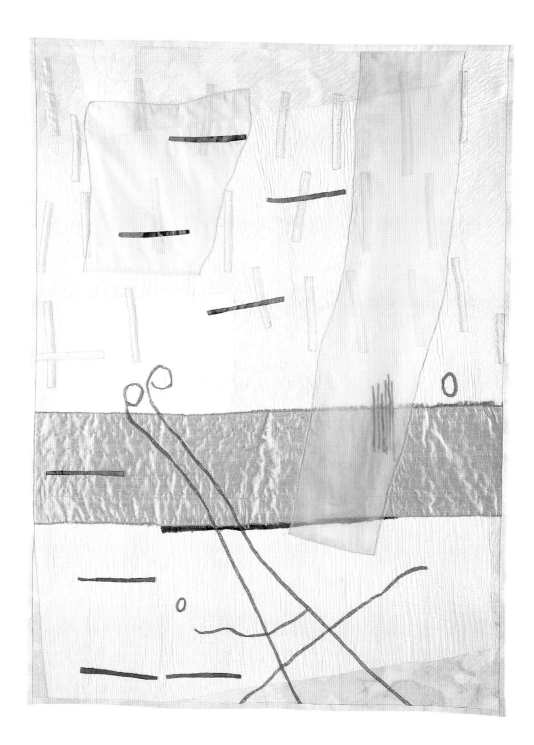

Rapture Silk, cotton, and polyester fabrics; machine appliquéd and quilted; 41 by 55 inches.

Space that encompasses endless views. White. Something shows through; it is not clear; is simple; is winter. Veiled, yet crisp. A path; to who knows where? Space you can breathe; is cool. It lifts.

Jeanne Lyons Butler
Huntington, New York

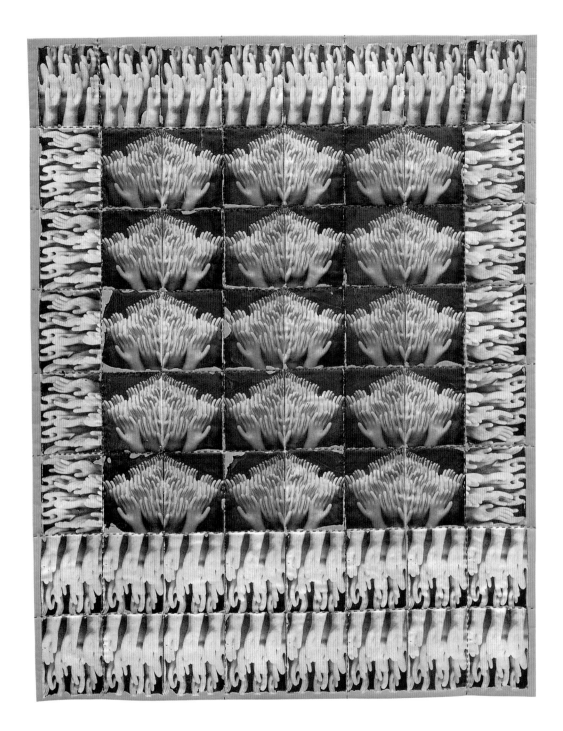

Hands Cotton cloth treated with textile paint and Polaroid transfers; hand stitched; 24 by 32 inches.

Hands is a whole cloth quilt that has been block printed with Polaroid film. It is part of a series of work called *Object Cloth*.

Melissa Holzinger
Arlington, Washington

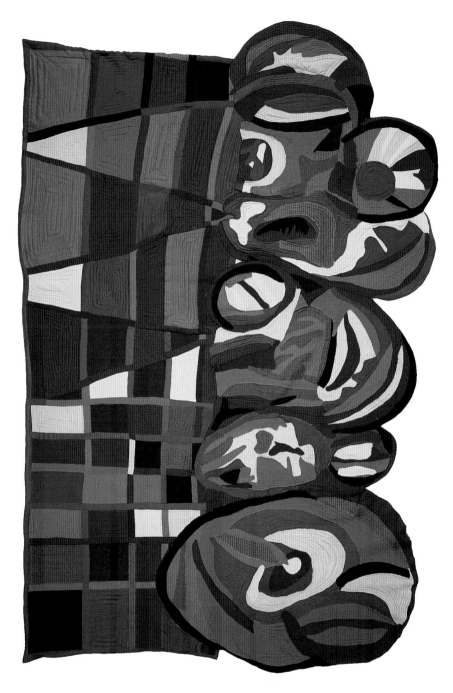

Harmony 100% cotton fabrics; direct appliqué, machine stitched; 64 by 104 inches

Shapes and structure give new character to the quilting picture. Vibrant feminine character (represented by the curving and circular shapes) joins in harmony with the more serious masculine character (represented by the square shapes).

Cvetka Hojnik-Dorojevič
Lendava, Slovenia

Rookie Award
sponsored by Studio Art Quilt Associates

After the Gold Rush Silk crepe de chine hand painted using acid dyes, water-based resist, salt, and alcohol techniques; machine quilted with monofilament and rayon threads; 26 by 21 inches.

Linda Gass
Los Altos, California

I grew up in California and have spent countless hours exploring the beauty of its mountains and deserts. In this quilt I have tried to beautify an unnatural landscape through a play of color and texture on silk. The landscape is I-5, a major transportation artery, crossing from the California Aqueduct, the man-made river that moves water from north to south and irrigates farm fields in what once was a desert. This is the second mining of California and hence the name of the quilt. (Inspired by a photograph by Ray Atkeson, courtesy of the Ray Atkeson Image Archive.)

Drop Zone Hand-dyed and commercial cottons, sheers, and decorative threads; reverse appliqué, sheer appliqué, machine embroidery, bobbin drawing, machine quilting; 63 by 63 inches.

When I make a quilt, I play with many elements: fabric, design, color, light, and threads. I delight in working without a net — no preplanning or drawing ahead of time. This keeps the quilt in progress alive and kicking.

Libby Lehman
Houston, Texas

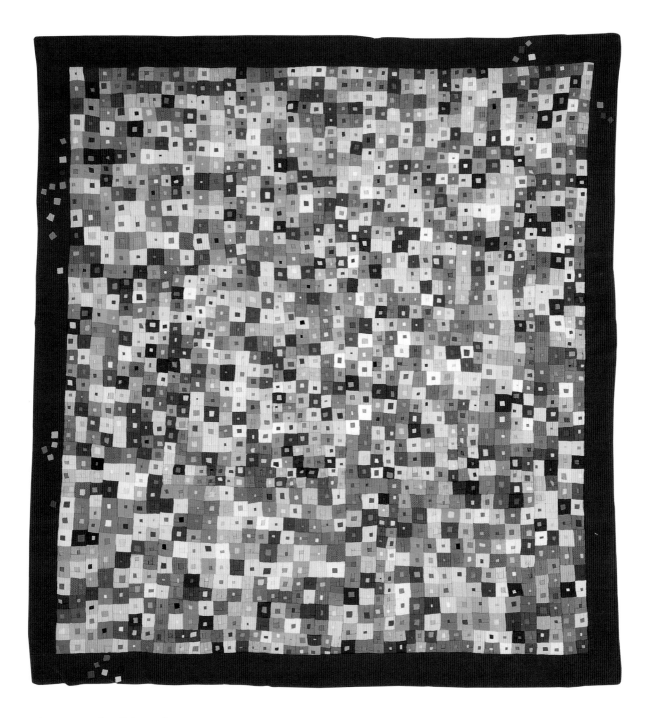

Colours in Disorder Commercial fabrics including cotton, blends, silk, and wool; pieced and appliquéd by machine and hand; hand quilted; 35 by 38 inches.

Colors have always been very important for me, and patchwork is a good way to play with them. I try to express my feelings and ideas with colors and simple forms.

Beatrice Lanter
Niederlenz, Switzerland

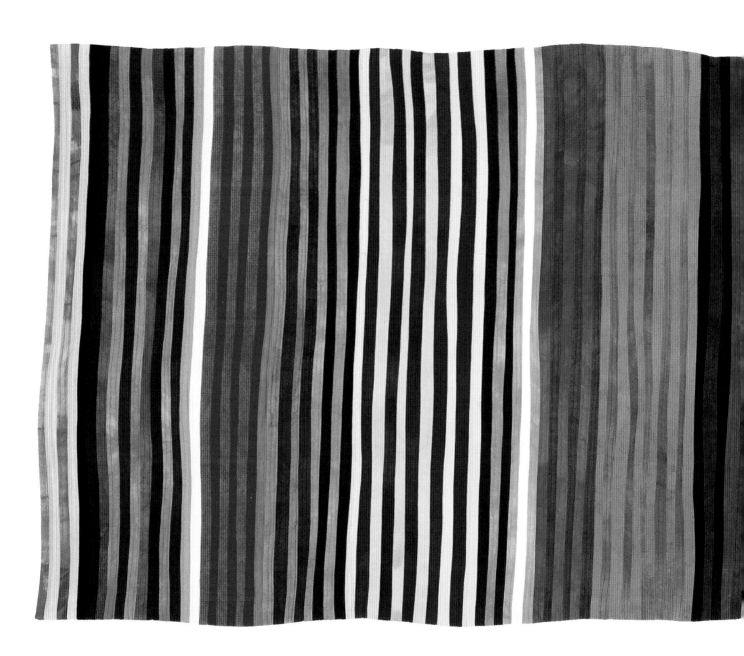

Color Study 2 Commercial and hand-dyed cottons; machine pieced and quilted; 87 by 35 inches.

Quilting provides a creative outlet that is grounded in family, community, and common experience, while offering unlimited problem solving, experimentation, and aesthetic range. I choose fabrics for their sensuality, tactile intimacy, familiarity, and tradition. Fabric has qualities of texture, light absorption, and reflection unmatched by any other medium. This quilt is an exploration of color interrelationships and line.

Eleanor A. McCain
Shalimar, Florida

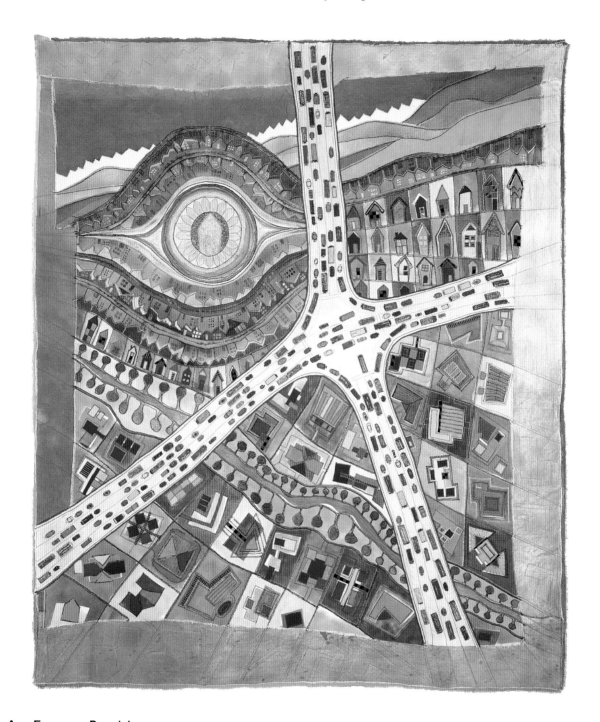

An Eye on Boulder Airbrushed canvas; fused, machine quilted, embroidered, and appliquéd; 60 by 71 inches.

Diana Bunnell
Boulder, Colorado

During my 40 years in Boulder, Colorado, I have seen many changes in the environment precipitated by growth. There is much competition for space in this small valley. Although our green belt policy has preserved many natural areas (including both banks of the creek that traverses the city), still the building continues, the traffic grows. I watch from the golden sanctuary of my home which dominates the landscape and is the center of the universe in my mind's eye.

The Patchy Memory of Roy G. Biv Cotton and blend fabrics and metallic and monofilament
thread; cyanotype printing, machine pieced, appliquéd, and quilted;
36 by 35 inches.

Marie Wohadlo
Chicago, Illinois

Life's commonalities are fleshed out in my work, which is often inspired by
family photo albums. I transmute snapshots into compositions of patchwork, appliqué, and embroidery. This process
strips photography of its heavy pretense to a specific reality into something more tactile and iconographic. Beyond
the appearance of immediacy and inherent suggestion of naiveté, my quiltwork is sandwiched with satire, commen-
tary, inquiry, and humor. Is it naive to believe that art can be tied to everyday experiences?

Natural Forces #3 Cotton fabrics; machine pieced and machine quilted; 53 by 58 inches.

My goal in this quilt was to get as much variety in rhythm and color as possible, while limiting the palette to only four fabrics. It is the third in a series of quilts inspired by the natural world, the elemental forces, growth, and regeneration.

Ann Schroeder
Jamaica Plain, Massachusetts

Juror's Award of Merit

A Sunny Day in April Hand-dyed and commercial cottons; machine appliquéd and machine quilted; 83 by 62 inches.

Emily Parson
St. Charles, Illinois

Last year, my husband and I bought our first house. Because we bought the house in the winter, we were unaware of the wonderful gardens planted by the previous owners. Spring was full of surprises, as hundreds of green shoots popped their heads through the snow. The profusion of tulips, combined with the happiness I was feeling in my new home, gave me a wonderful new enthusiasm for my work.

Blue Fish Cotton duck fabric and woven hemp treated with oil stick, acrylic, and fabric paint; photo silkscreen, color copy transfer, machine stitching; 52 by 68 inches.

My work evolves intuitively as I draw from the images of my personal photography. Accidents are incorporated and appreciated in the form of creases and torn areas. I hope to create an internal landscape which captures the essence of nature.

Fran Skiles
Plantation, Florida

Some Heaven Some Earth No.1 Commercially and hand-dyed cotton, cotton blend, and silk fabrics; machine pieced and machine quilted; 43 by 80 inches.

Odette Tolksdorf
Durban, Kwazulu-Natal, South Africa

Three ideas came together as my starting point: first, the desire to explore the use of sinuous, curved lines (rather than shape); second, thoughts of integration; and third, the desire to create an impression of landscape. The design is a metaphor of my hopes for South Africa. In the upper area, narrow wavy lines enter in isolated groups with a sense of uncertainty. As they move lower down, they gradually start integrating with the other elements until they form a cohesive unity.

Wolfwomen Hand-dyed cotton, airbrushed, stamped, and drawn; hand and machine pieced and appliquéd, hand quilted; 54 by 58 inches.

Listening to our inner *Wolfwomen*, we experience wisdom and intuition. Inspired by a book by Clarissa Pinkola Estés.

Gudrun Bechet
Dudelange, Luxembourg

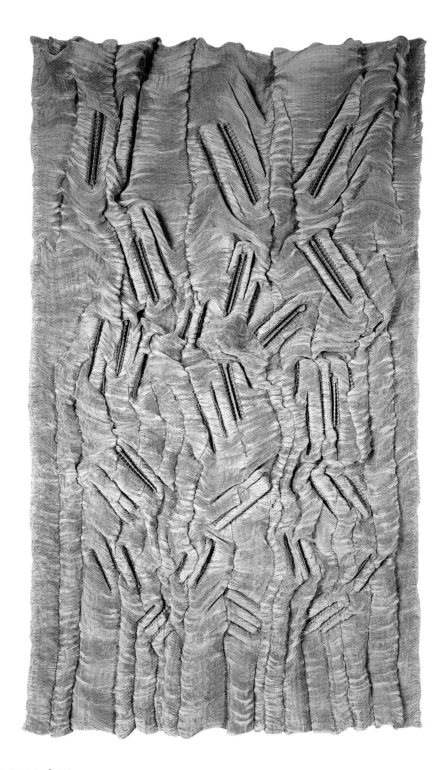

Wrapped Grid / Blue Hand painted and pleated silk, shaped rug canvas; shaped and tied with silk threads; 28 by 49 inches.

In my recent work I have been exploring ways of making the inner (batting) layer more evident. The idea for the forms in this piece developed after watching a film about pillow lava forming underwater from fissures in the contorted sea floor.

Ardyth Davis
Reston, Virginia

The Best in Contemporary Quilts

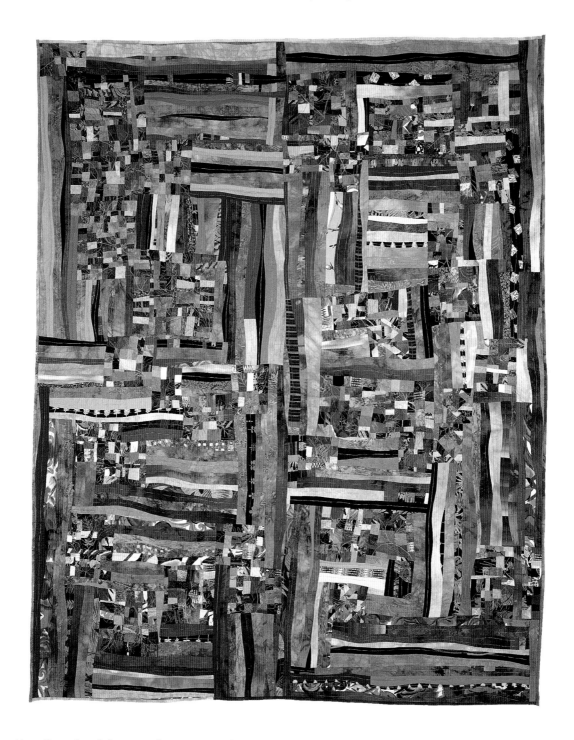

In the Smoky Mountains Cotton fabric and batting; machine pieced and quilted; 71 by 90 inches.

This quilt was inspired by a trip through the Smoky Mountains and the beautiful diffused colors of those mountains. The quilting design was taken from the shrubs and trees growing in the area.

Jutta Farringer
Constantia Cape, South Africa

Persiennes Silk and cotton fabrics; machine pieced using the paper piecing method and machine quilted; 45 by 63 inches.

Odile Texier
Saint-Aunes, France

I am fascinated by geometric lines, light, colors, and fabrics. Silk is my favorite fabric, as it shines and lives at the same time. I was born in Lyon, France — the capital of silk — and silk inspired me to create *Persiennes*. (*Persiennes* means Venetian shutters in French.) The quilt reminds me of the times in my childhood when I enjoyed the light coming through my room's shutters.

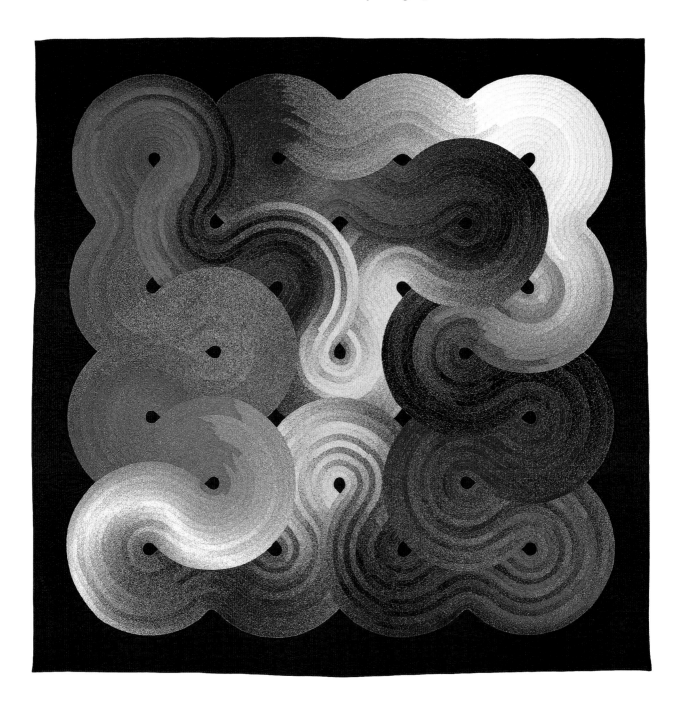

Waves #4 Cotton fabrics; machine pieced, appliquéd, and quilted; 77 by 77 inches.

This work is an outcome of a sudden flash of inspiration which struck me while trying to find out how these fabrics could be used to make this design more effective. These waves are like life. Sometimes it's bright and delightful, sometimes gloomy and difficult. But hope always shines again; it reflects my life as a quilter.

Etsuko Takahashi
Yokohama, Japan

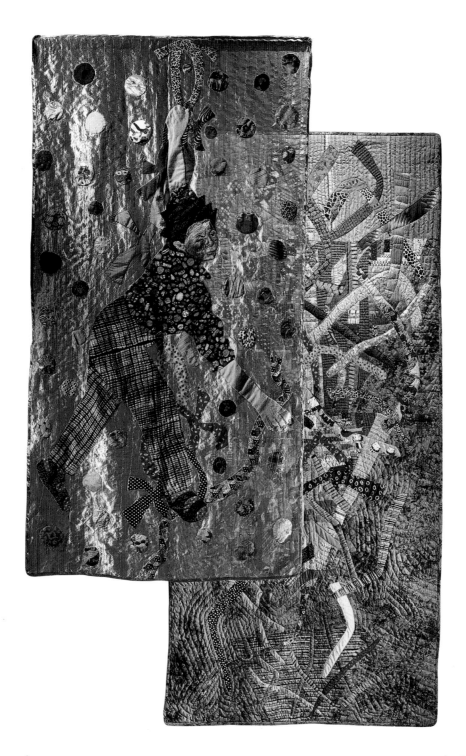

The Struggle Silk (metallic and other) and cotton fabrics, cotton embroidery thread; 42 by 80 inches (left) and 48 by 98 inches (right).

In the dream, the only way down the stairwell was by a strip ladder.
As I nervously edged out onto the slipping, knotted–cloth assemblage,
I noticed that the only way to proceed was to grab another strip and tie it on.

Terrie Hancock
Cincinnati, Ohio

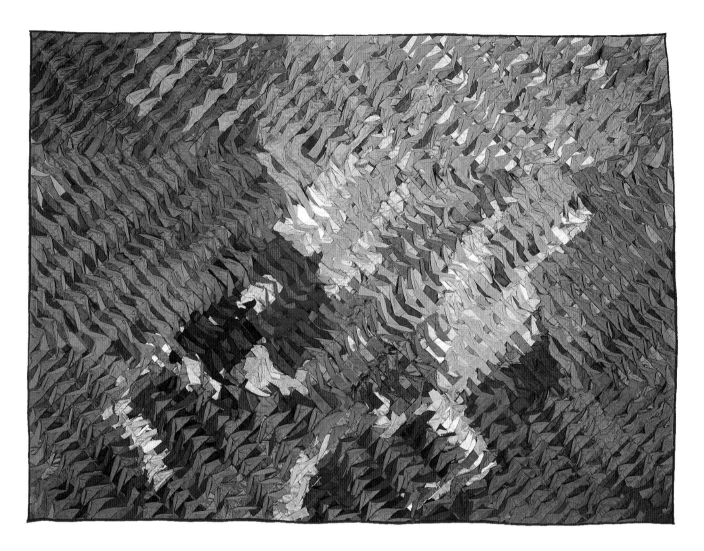

Swimmers Silk and cotton duck fabrics; reverse appliqué, layered, stitched, cut, restitched, and cut again; 80 by 60 inches.

Tim Harding
Stillwater, Minnesota

In an effort to unify form with content, the representation of two underwater swimmers in a pool is partially obscured — but also revealed — by my reverse appliqué method. This accomplishes an abstracted, broken-up image somewhat like the refraction of light that occurs in water. I use an iridescent silk which is reflective, like water. The surface texture is a broken-up wave pattern such as you might see in a pool. A slight use of perspective is accomplished by a subtle foreshortening of the torsos and elongation of the arms. Light/shadow and figure/ground relationships are also used to create the illusion of depth.

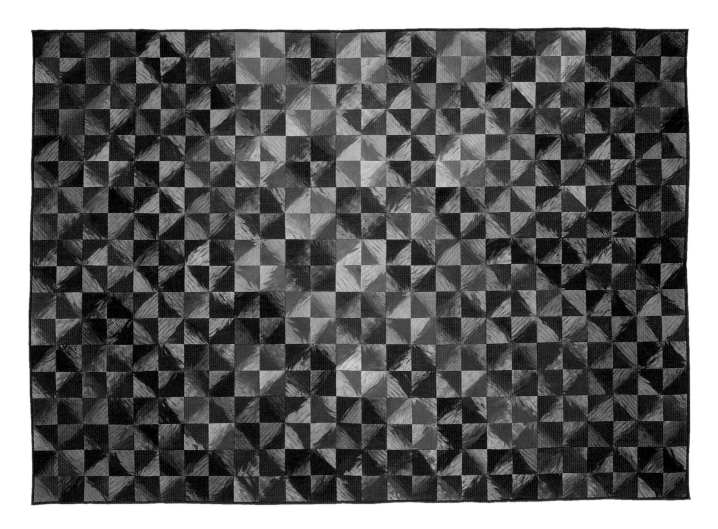

Grandmothers' Influence 100% cotton fabric Shibori dyed in Procion dyes with multiple immersions; machine pieced and quilted; 88 by 62 inches.

This quilt is in honor of our grandmothers, who, in their respective ways, taught us the beginnings of our art. Debra's grandmother taught her to sew four-patch quilts as a child, while Michael's grandmother taught him jewelry making and gem cutting at an early age. We thank them both for their vision.

Debra Lunn and
Michael Mrowka
Lancaster, Ohio

About the Dairy Barn

The Dairy Barn Southeastern Ohio Cultural Arts Center is a unique arts facility in the Appalachian foothills. It has showcased regional, national, and international arts and crafts since 1978, and offers a year-round calendar of events featuring international juried exhibits, programs and exhibits of regional interest, festivals, performances, special activities and arts education classes for children and adults.

The history of the Dairy Barn is as colorful as its exhibits. Built in 1913, the structure housed an active dairy herd until the late 1960s. Ten years later, local artist Harriet Anderson and her banker-philanthropist husband Ora recognized the building's potential as a much-needed regional arts center, and they worked tirelessly to rally community support to save the idle, dilapidated structure. With only nine days to spare, the demolition order was reversed. The building was placed on the National Register of Historic Places, and the Dairy Barn Southeastern Ohio Cultural Arts Center was born.

Through several renovation projects, the architects retained the original character of the building as it evolved from a seasonal, makeshift exhibit space into a first-class, fully-accessible arts facility with a 7,000-square-foot gallery that also includes the specially equipped Ann Howland Arts Education Center. A 1.1 million dollar renovation and expansion project to make the facility a full-service arts center is currently in progress. When completed in the year 2000, the Barn will have five new classrooms, one additional gallery, a catering kitchen/receiving area, an atrium, and a gift shop. In 1995, the Dairy Barn received a $65,000 State of Ohio grant that

4Quilt National '97 installations.

will enable the start of the ultimate transformation of the upper level for an additional classroom, a meeting area, an auxiliary gallery, an artist-in-residence studio, an exhibit preparation space, and an always-needed storage area.

The Dairy Barn is supported by admissions, memberships, corporate sponsorships, grants, and donations. The staff is assisted by a large group of volunteers who annually donate thousands of hours of time and talent. For a calendar of events and information about other Dairy Barn programs, contact the Dairy Barn Arts Center, P.O. Box 747, Athens, Ohio, 45701 USA; phone 614/592-4981; or visit the World Wide Web site at *http://www.dairybarn.org*.

Show Itinerary

The complete **Quilt National '99** collection will be on display from May 29 through September 6, 1999 at the Dairy Barn Southeastern Ohio Cultural Arts Center, 8000 Dairy Lane, Athens, Ohio. Three separate groups of **Quilt National '99** works [identified as A, B, and C] will then begin a two-year tour of museums and galleries. Host venues will display only a portion of the full Quilt National '99 collection.

Tentative dates and locations are listed below. For an updated itinerary or to receive additional information about hosting a Quilt National touring collection, contact the Dairy Barn Cultural Arts Center, P.O. Box 747, Athens, Ohio, 45701-0747. Phone: 740-592-4981. FAX: 740-592-5090. E-MAIL: info@dairybarn.org. World Wide Web site: http://www.dairybarn.org.

10/1 - 11/15/99   *St Louis, MO*
The City Museum [full touring collection]

3/4 - 5/13/2000   *Pueblo, CO*
Sangre de Cristo Arts and Conference Center [C]

4/6 - 4/9/2000   *Lancaster, PA*
Quilters' Heritage Celebration [A & B]

5/12 - 7/23/2000   *Rock Hill, SC*
Museum of York County [A]

5/12 - 7/2/2000   *York, SC*
Charlotte (NC) Quilt Guild [B]

9/16 - 10/29/2000   *Saginaw, MI*
Saginaw Art Museum [B]

10/1 - 10/31/2000   *Waverly, IA*
Wartburg College, Waldemar A. Schmidt Gallery [A]

11/14/2000 - 2/25/01   *Abingdon, VA*
William King Regional Arts Center [A]

11/2/2000 - 1/6/01   *Columbus, OH*
Riffe Gallery [C]

1/7 - 3/11/01   *Fort Dodge, IA*
Blanden Memorial Art Museum [B]

Contact the Dairy Barn Cultural Arts Center for additional bookings. It is recommended that you verify this information by calling a specific host venue prior to visiting the site.

Artists' Index

Marjorie Hoeltzel
St. Louis, Missouri
Cacophony
Page 75

Cvetka Hojnik-Dorojevič
Lendava, Slovinija
Harmony
Page 88

Melissa Holzinger
Arlintgon, Washington
Hands
Page 87

Judy Hooworth
New South Wales, Australia
*Mothers/Daughters #6: Lines of
Communication*
Page 66

Inge Hueber
Köln, Germany
Ikat Quilt / Rhythm II
Page 70

Donna Leigh Jackins
Birmingham, Alabama
Laissez-Les Manger du Pizza
Page 71

Janis V. Jagodzinski
Baltimore, Maryland
Sea Goddess
Page 28

Melody Johnson
Cary, Illinois
Aquifer
Page 47

Harue Konishi
Tokyo, Japan
Miyabi
Page 17

Beatrice Lanter
Niederlenz, Switzerland
Colours In Disorder
Page 91

Judith Larzelere
Belmont, Massachusetts
Tumbling Reds
Page 43

John W. Lefelhocz
Athens, Ohio
Money for Nothing
Page 76

Libby Lehman
Houston, Texas
Drop Zone
Page 90

Linda Levin
Wayland, Massachusetts
Maine / Frenchman's Bay II
Page 15

Jane Lloyd
Ballymena, County Antrim,
Northern Ireland
Trick Track
Page 60

Vita Marie Lovett
Marietta, Georgia
Primitive Door Series - VIII Keep Out
Page 51

Debra Lunn and Michael Mrowka
Lancaster, Ohio
Grandmothers' Influence
Page 107

Linda MacDonald
Willits, California
Town News
Page 79

Eleanor A. McCain
Shalimar, Florida
Color Study 2
Page 92

Judy McDermott
Thornleigh, New South Wales,
Australia
A Real Pretend Wagga for Paul Klee
Page 81

Barbara Barrick McKie
Lyme, Connecticut
Floral Symphony #2: Foxgloves
Page 57

Ann Stamm Merrell
Cupertino, California
Celtic Crosses 3.1, 3.2, 3.3
Page 52

Jan Myers-Newbury
Pittsburgh, Pennsylvania
Agape
Page 48

Dominie Nash
Bethesda, Maryland
Red Landscape 2
Page 42

Miriam Nathan-Roberts
Berkeley, California
Spin Cycle
Page 32

Anne McKenzie Nickolson
Indianapolis, Indiana
In Perspective
Page 63

Sara Nissim
Ramat-Gan, Israel
Hamsa
Page 59

Alice Norman
Boise, Idaho
57 Bel Air Coupe
Page 33

Pat Owoc
St. Louis, Missouri
Earth and Soul "To Go"
Page 27

Jill Pace
Glendale, Arizona
Tutti Frutti
Page 56